AF571722

CRIPPLE CREEK RAILROADS

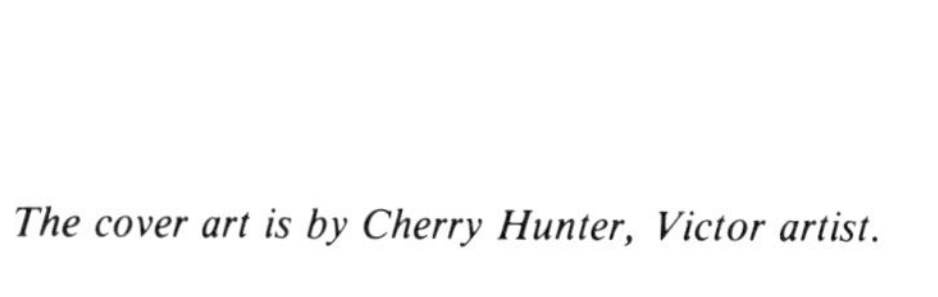

The cover art is by Cherry Hunter, Victor artist.

CRIPPLE CREEK RAILROADS

A Quick History of the Great Gold Camp's Railroads

By

LELAND FEITZ

Published by
LITTLE LONDON PRESS
380 No. Limit
Colorado Springs, Colorado 80904

Copyright 1968
By
LELAND FEITZ

Library of Congress Card Number 68-3079

Twelfth Printing, March 1991

INTRODUCTION

by

TED S. MCKEE
Pine Valley, Colorado

Past President of the Rocky Mountain Railroad Club

No story of early Colorado could be written without at least passing mention of the railroads which plunged into the state's mountain vastness at scores of points. The lines wound along on narrow shelf roadbeds hacked out of canyon walls, climbed to dizzying heights above timberline, roared through networks of tunnels, cuts and fills, each an engineering marvel.

For it was the railroads that brought people into this raw land ... farmers, cattlemen, merchants, miners and madams ... and it was the railroads that carried the rich ores out of the mountains to reach the markets of the world. And because the railroads reached slim, sometimes precarious steel fingers into canyons and on to peaks, Colorado was able to develop and prosper more rapidly and systematically than any other western state.

The study of these early railroads is both rewarding and fascinating. Buffs have literally devoted lifetimes to reading, searching for old photos, tramping abandoned roadbeds and eagerly collecting artifacts as they reach back through time to learn the story of the little engines and big men who built the state of Colorado. The result is one of the best documented and thoroughly researched histories in the country today. Near Golden, Colorado, there is an entire museum devoted solely to the state's rail history.

Yet with all this excellent research material, there is a serious gap: few, if any, popular references have been written for the casual reader. The traveler, resident or tourist, who simply wants to know a little bit about the highway he is driving, is curious about what is obviously a railroad station (sans railroad) in the middle of nowhere, or who answers, "You've got to be kidding!" when told that streetcars once operated at nearly 11,000 feet delivering miners to their diggings.

Leland Feitz has taken a giant step toward filling that gap. This volume supplies the answers to many questions about the railroads of Cripple Creek, quickly, succinctly and certainly in adequate detail for the average reader. Mr. Feitz, as a parttime resident of Cripple Creek, is qualified to provide this information.

Travel now back into a history filled with chuffing steam engines, hardrock miners, construction feats unequalled in railroad annals, and people with a mighty dream and the sheer guts to make it come true.

Until the trains came, stage lines connected Cripple Creek with the towns of Florissant and Divide on the Colorado Midland Railway. (Collection of Ray Ziegler)

The old Palace Hotel in Cripple Creek where the stages loaded and unloaded.

BEFORE THE TRAINS CAME

After Bob Womack discovered gold in Poverty Gulch in 1890, people by the thousands poured into the Cripple Creek-Victor mining district in central Colorado. Even by 1894 when the first passenger train arrived in Cripple Creek there were already some 20,000 people living in the great gold camp. Over 175 gold mines were already operating.

Until the arrival of that first passenger train, stage lines provided fast, frequent, and dependable service between the Cripple Creek district and the towns of Divide and Florissant some twenty miles north of the gold camp. At these points, the stage lines connected with the Colorado Midland Railroad for points west and for Colorado Springs and Denver.

The Hundley Stage was one of the first and the District's most popular line. Hundley ran two coaches in and out of Cripple Creek every day of the week. They carried up to twelve passengers. Three teams of horses pulled each coach over the rough mountain roads between the mining camp and the railroad.

One stage left Cripple Creek every morning at eight o'clock. It connected with a train in Divide which arrived in Colorado Springs at two-thirty in the afternoon and in Denver at six o'clock.

By leaving the mining camp on the two-thirty afternoon stage, early day travelers could be in Colorado Springs at eight twenty-five that evening or in Denver before midnight.

There were also longer, slower stage and freight roads from Cripple Creek and Victor to Florence and Canon City. Connections were made at these two cities with the Denver & Rio Grande Railroad.

Stage service and wagon freighting between the mining camp and outside cities ended after the arrival of the Florence & Cripple Creek and Midland Terminal Railroads. However, both services continued within the District itself until the railway network was completed there.

The Cripple Creek District's first train was the narrow gauge Florence & Cripple Creek. It approached the gold camp over these steep grades just south of Victor. (Denver Public Library Western Collection)

On leaving the mining district, the Florence & Cripple Creek dropped down into rugged Phantom Canyon over a series of spectacular loops. (Denver Public Library Western Collection)

THE FLORENCE & CRIPPLE CREEK

"The Gold Belt Line"

The gold camp's first train arrived in Cripple Creek on July 1, 1894. It was the narrow gauge Florence & Cripple Creek Railroad, one of the shortest lived but most successful railroads ever built.

From Florence, forty miles south of the gold camp, the Florence & Cripple Creek steamed up Phantom Canyon to Victor, through the towns of Elkton and Anaconda, and on to Cripple Creek over steep, winding grades. It was a climb to just under 10,000 feet from a starting elevation of 5,187 feet.

Known as "The Gold Belt Line," the Florence & Cripple Creek operated three passenger trains each way on a daily schedule between Florence and Cripple Creek. They connected with the Denver & Rio Grande at Florence.

Overnight Pullman service was available between Cripple Creek and Denver. Each night at nine o'clock, a train left Cripple Creek's Florence & Cripple Creek depot for the capital city. At one-thirty every morning, another Pullman train left Colorado Springs for the gold camp.

The Florence & Cripple Creek also ran as many as fifty-eight passenger trains a day between Cripple Creek and Victor. And its narrow gauge subsidiary company, the Golden Circle, reached out from Victor into the rich mining fields for the very profitable ore shipments.

At one time, the Florence & Cripple Creek boasted over 300 freight cars and sixteen passenger coaches. Its locomotives were named for regional landmarks, gold mines, and individuals connected with the camp. The number one locomotive was the *Victor* followed by the *Cripple Creek, Elkton, Anaconda, W. S. Stratton, Goldfield, Gold Coin, Portland, Vindicator, Strong, Last Dollar,* etc.

The Florence & Cripple Creek was a tremendously successful railroad, paying for itself during its first year of operation. But it had a short life. The end came in 1912 when a flash flood hit Phantom Canyon and wiped out nine miles of right-of-way and eighteen bridges.

Anaconda was one of several mining towns between Cripple Creek and Victor to be served by the Florence & Cripple Creek. (State Historical Society of Colorado)

Wreck of the Florence & Cripple Creek near Anaconda, July 2, 1894, one day after the arrival of the gold camp's first train. (State Historical Society of Colorado)

The Florence & Cripple Creek depot at Cripple Creek, elevation 9,493 feet.

The District's yards for the Florence & Cripple Creek Railroad were in Victor just below the rich Strong Mine.

The Florence & Cripple Creek provided daily Pullman service between Cripple Creek and Colorado Springs, Pueblo and Denver.

Coach interior on the "Cripple Creek Limited." (State Historical Society of Colorado)

THE MIDLAND TERMINAL

"Historic Ute Indian Trail Route"

The gold camp's second railroad was the standard gauge Midland Terminal. It reached the District on July 4, 1894, just three days after the Florence & Cripple Creek reached Cripple Creek town. However, it was December of 1895 before the Midland Terminal's tracks reached Cripple Creek and the line started operating passenger trains between there and Colorado Springs. In the meantime, Midland Terminal trains were met at Gillett and Cameron by stage coaches which rushed travelers into Cripple Creek.

The Midland Terminal traveled west up Ute Pass over the Colorado Midland as far as Divide. There it headed south for Gillett through rugged mountain country. Then it continued on to Cameron, over Victor Pass, and into Victor. It passed through Elkton and Anaconda before it reached the big three-story brick depot at the foot of Bennett Avenue in Cripple Creek.

It was fifty-five miles from Colorado Springs (elevation 5,992) to Cripple Creek (elevation 9,493). The trip took just over two hours and a round trip coach ticket cost $2.50.

The Midland Terminal ran four passenger trains each way every day between Colorado Springs and Cripple Creek. The "Cripple Creek Flyer" provided daily through sleeper service between the gold camp and Denver.

Those headed for the District could leave Colorado Springs every morning at three thirty, eight fifty-five or eleven fifteen, or they could take a late afternoon train. Trains left Cripple Creek every morning at two forty and every afternoon at two twenty-five, six thirty or eight fifteen.

As long as the District's gold ore had to be hauled to the processing mill in Colorado Springs, the Midland Terminal held on as a freight line. The building of the Carlton Mill in the District in 1949 eliminated any need for rail service and that year the Midland Terminal passed from the scene.

The Midland Terminal approached the depot at Cripple Creek over Poverty Gulch near the spot where Bob Womack discovered gold in 1890 and started the last of the great gold rushes. (Denver Public Library Western Collection)

During the boom years, the Midland Terminal ran four passenger trains each way each day between Colorado Springs and Cripple Creek. (Denver Public Library Western Collection)

Gillett was the District's "gateway" city. This was the Midland Terminal depot there.

Victor's Midland Terminal depot was destroyed in 1899 by a fire which nearly leveled the entire city. (State Historical Society of Colorado)

Beyond the Goldfield Depot the LaBella Power Plant and the Golden Cycle Mine can be seen. Goldfield with a population of about 3,500 was the District's third biggest city.

The Midland Terminal's main yards were in Colorado Springs near the giant Golden Cycle Mill where Cripple Creek's gold ore was processed. (Denver Public Library Western Collection, Photo by Ernest S. Peyton)

With Pikes Peak in the background, a train load of gold ore is seen headed for the mill in Colorado Springs. Armed guards often rode down with the rich ore shipments.

As late as January of 1949, the Midland Terminal was still hauling great loads of gold ore out of the Cripple Creek District. (Denver Public Library Western Collection)

After serving the gold camp for over half a century, the Midland Terminal was forced to end operations in 1949. This was the last passenger train to leave Cripple Creek. (Denver Public Library Western Collection)

Wrecking crews went to work ripping up the Midland Terminal tracks soon after the last run was made in 1949. (Denver Public Library Western Collection)

THE COLORADO SPRINGS & CRIPPLE CREEK DISTRICT

"The Short Line"

It was over five years after the arrival of the Midland Terminal before the third railroad reached Cripple Creek from the plains below. This was the standard gauge Colorado Springs & Cripple Creek District Railway. It operated two passenger trains each way every day between the two cities beginning in April of 1901.

This line offered the most direct service to the gold fields, for it struck out right over the hills from Colorado Springs. It reached Cripple Creek in nine fewer miles than the Midland Terminal and became known as the Short Line.

Built by rich Cripple Creek mine owners, the forty-six mile road cost just over $4,500,000. Its rolling stock included eight 85-ton locomotives, four switch engines, eighteen passenger cars, four observation cars, 225 box cars, and sixty ore cars.

From the start, the Short Line was considered a marvel of railroad engineering and fast became the popular way to Cripple Creek and one of the state's great tourist attractions. Theodore Roosevelt rode the Short Line in 1901 and exclaimed: "This is the ride that bankrupts the English language!" During the following summer, well over 50,000 tourists traveled over the new line.

Competition for passengers was keen after the coming of the Short Line. Right after it began operating, the Midland Terminal dropped its round-trip Colorado Springs-Cripple Creek fare to $2, to $1.50 and then to $1. The Short Line met the rates. Then the Midland Terminal dropped its fare to fifty cents and the Short Line answered with a twenty-five cent round-trip ticket before a truce was reached.

Like the Florence & Cripple Creek, the Short Line did not have a very long life. Only four years after it started operating, it had to be sold to escape receivership. The Colorado & Southern was the buyer and it immediately leased it to the Midland Terminal. Service over the Short Line to Cripple Creek ended in 1920.

Building the Short Line at the turn of the century. It was the last railroad to be built to the District. (State Historical Society of Colorado)

One of the steeper grades on the Cripple Creek Short Line. The standard gauge road served the gold camp from 1901 until 1920.

Three elevations of track on the Cripple Creek Short Line. (Colorado Springs Chamber of Commerce)

From Point Sublime on the Short Line, passengers had a magnificent view of the city of Colorado Springs, Broadmoor, and the plains. The "X" indicates where the Broadmoor Hotel complex now stands. (Denver Public Library Western Collection)

One of many trestles over which Short Line trains passed on their spectacular climb from the plains to the gold camp. (State Historical Society of Colorado)

Two Short Line trains meeting on top Hoosier Pass (elevation 10,314 feet) just above Cripple Creek. (State Historical Society of Colorado)

One of the Short Line's two daily passenger trains climbing up toward the gold camp. Colorado Springs can be seen on the plains below. (Colorado Springs Chamber of Commerce)

A Short Line passenger train within the mining district, about midway between Cripple Creek and Victor.

STREET CARS

In addition to the fast and frequent passenger trains that operated within the District, there were two electric streetcar systems providing day and night service to the cities and principal mines. They were known as the High Line and the Low Line.

The High Line, the highest interurban railroad in North America, made a twelve-mile run between downtown Cripple Creek and downtown Victor by way of Midway (elevation 10,487), Independence, and Goldfield. High Line cars operated on the hour between five o'clock each morning and two o'clock each night.

The Low Line also connected the District's two big cities and served Elkton and Anaconda. Low Line trains ran every thirty minutes over this five-mile track. The fare was five cents.

The streetcars, for the most part, operated over the rails of the Colorado Springs & Cripple Creek District Railway, and like that system, they stopped operating in 1920.

The little cars were built to seat forty passengers. However, during changes of shifts, when traffic was heavy, they often carried as many as 100 miners.

For almost a quarter of a century, the cities of the Cripple Creek District were linked together by two electric interurban systems known as the High Line and the Low Line. This turn-of-the-century drawing indicates the routes the street cars took. (Denver Public Library Western Collection)

When Cripple Creek was Colorado's fourth biggest city, street cars operated on its principal streets. This was Bennett Avenue in 1908.

In 1900 Victor had a population of over 18,000. It was tied to the District's other cities with two street car systems. (Collection of Fred and Jo Mazzulla)

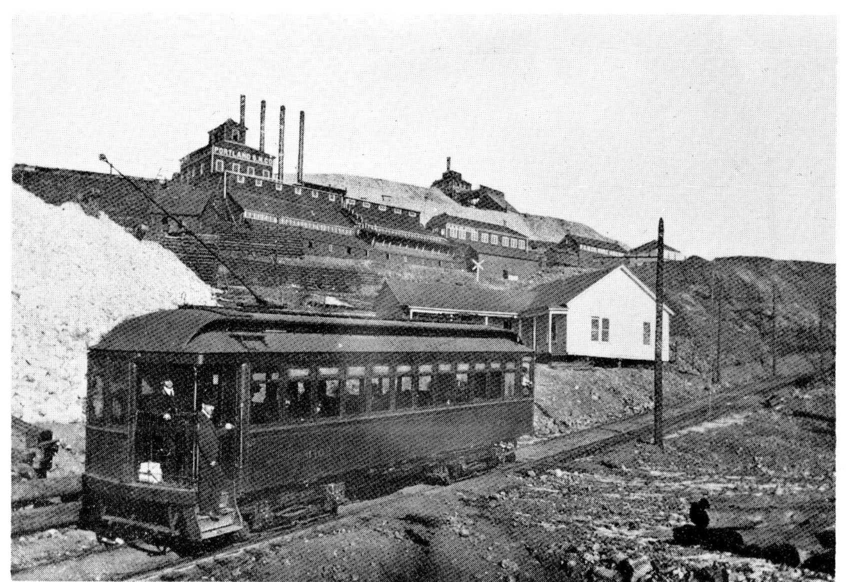

The electric cars made regular stops at the principal mines. This was a High Line car on Battle Mountain above Victor at the Portland Mine, the District's greatest producer. (Pioneer Museum, Colorado Springs)

For five cents miners could ride the little electric cars from the heart of the camp's cities to the gold mines where they worked. (Denver Public Library Western Collection)

After the abandonment of the Midland Terminal in 1949, Colorado built a new highway to Cripple Creek over the old railroad grade.

The last train passed through this tunnel in 1949. Months later, cars were traveling through it.

AFTERWARDS

After the railroads were dismantled, most of the old grades were turned into auto highways. The first to be converted was the roadbed of the Florence & Cripple Creek.

As early as 1914 the Victor Auto Club recommended that the Florence & Cripple Creek grade be worked over and opened as an auto road. But it was 1918 before the State of Colorado actually opened the Phantom Canyon Highway to auto traffic.

The road connects Victor with US Highway 50 a few miles east of Canon City. It is one of the most scenic roads into the gold camp, safe but very slow.

Colorado State Highway 67 uses several miles of the Midland Terminal roadbed between Divide and Cripple Creek. The highway takes to the old railroad grade just above Rainbow Valley. It passes through a Midland Terminal tunnel and continues on over railroad grades as far as the ghost town of Gillett.

This is a good, all-weather road and the most popular route into the Cripple Creek District. That part of it which uses the Midland Terminal grades was opened soon after the line's abandonment in 1949.

In 1924, the Corley Mountain Highway opened over what had been the Short Line road. It operated as a toll road until 1939. Now called the Gold Camp Road, it is another slow but exceedingly scenic drive between Colorado Springs and Cripple Creek. The road still passes through seven of the nine Short Line tunnels.

Another highway of interest is Colorado State 143 between Florissant and Cripple Creek. It follows the route of the old stage road which connected the gold camp with the Colorado Midland Railroad. Though not paved, it is a good road and is traveled all year.

Within the District itself many miles of railroad grades have been turned into highways and jeep roads.

Automobiles have been passing over the Florence & Cripple Creek grades since 1918 when the scenic Phantom Canyon Road was opened. Even today many of the old railroad bridges, trestles, and tunnels are still in use.

In 1924, the Corley Mountain Highway, a toll road to Cripple Creek, opened over what had been the Short Line roadbed. It passes over the Short Line's trestles and through seven of the railroad's nine tunnels. (Colorado Springs Chamber of Commerce)

It was no freeway, but the Corley Mountain Highway was one of the West's most beautiful drives. The road has been improved over the years and is now the Gold Camp Road. (Colorado Springs Chamber of Commerce)

Colorado State Highway 67 now passes through this old Midland Terminal Railroad tunnel between Divide and Cripple Creek.

Early day motorists paid $1.00 each to travel up the Corley Mountain Highway to Cripple Creek. Now it is a free road.

THE CRIPPLE CREEK AND VICTOR NARROW GAUGE

Seventy-three years after the first railroad arrived in the Cripple Creek District another narrow gauge has appeared on the scene. It is the Cripple Creek & Victor Narrow Gauge and it started operating during the summer of 1967 as a tourist attraction.

The little train leaves from the old depot at the end of Bennett Avenue and continues south over Midland Terminal grades.

Vista Grande, the locomotive pictured below, weighs only fifteen tons. Before being brought to Cripple Creek it was in use by a mining company near Monterey, Mexico. It was built in Pittsburgh in 1927.

The gay little cars are the open observation type to give the rider the full benefit of steam railroading in the high, historic mining country.

Cripple Creek's newest tourist attraction, the Cripple Creek and Victor Narrow Gauge. It started operating in 1967. (The Cripple Creek Gold Rush)

For those who want more detailed information about the Cripple Creek District and its railroads, the following books are suggested:

Cafky, Morris. *Rails Around Gold Hill.* Rocky Mountain Railroad Club, 1955.

Beebe & Clegg. *Narrow Gauge in the Rockies.* Howell-North Press, 1958.

Sprague, Marshall. *Money Mountain.* Little Brown & Co., 1953.

Lathrop, Gilbert. *Little Engines and Big Men.* Caxton, 1954.

Taylor, Robert Guilford. *Cripple Creek.* Indiana University Publications, 1967.

These books were helpful in writing this quick history of the Cripple Creek District's railroads as were Cripple Creek's early newspapers, the *Cripple Creek Gold Rush,* and the *Colorado Springs Gazette.*

Cripple Creek's excellent museum was once the Midland Terminal Railroad Station.

By the same author

CRIPPLE CREEK!

A Quick History of the World's Greatest Gold Camp

MYERS AVENUE

A Quick History of Cripple Creek's Red-Light District

VICTOR

A Quick History of Colorado's "City of Mines"

PLATORO

Mining Camp & Resort Town